THE STORY
OF
Rob
ROY

CORBIE

Chapter One

Let us go on a raid with Rob Roy MacGregor. It is autumn in 1690 and he is twenty years old. It is a grim time, and he is an angry young man. His father is in prison in Edinburgh. The proceeds of the harvest have been seized by the government. Winter is approaching, and without food or money, the MacGregors will starve. It is the end of September now, when the black cattle are on the move, being driven south along the drove roads before winter freezes the mountains.

The MacGregors have eyes and ears everywhere along the Highland Line. Rob Roy knows that a great herd of cattle, belonging to Sir Alexander Livingston, is being driven east to Stirling. Sir Alexander is no friend of the Highlanders, so his cattle are fair game. Up before sunrise, fifty fierce-looking young men in belted plaids and armed with long swords and daggers join Rob Roy at the meeting place. Their feet bare or in light home-made shoes, they speedily cover the grass and heather, wading rivers, until after about twelve miles they come out from the hills. Past the village of Aberfoyle is the wide, flat marshy ground called Flanders Moss. Here there is a broad earth-and-grass track along which the herds of cattle are driven.

Still early in the day, they reach Buchlyvie, a straggling line of low thatched cottages. They wait. For the villagers, in their houses and fields, to see the arrival of a band of armed Highlanders is a nightmare come true. Fearing the worst, they send their own speediest men running to the next villages, south to Balfron and east to Kippen, to give warning and get help. But the Highlanders simply wait among the houses. Rob Roy has no quarrel with the villagers.

But the villagers, alarmed and fearful, gather their numbers and, armed with their own farm tools, scythes, sticks and cudgels, shout to the raiders to get out of the village. Not wanting to provoke a fight, Rob Roy takes his men out from the shelter of the houses on to the rising ground of Kippen Muir, from where he can look out for the cattle coming The farmers, perhaps thinking that the clansmen have been scared off, follow them up on to the Muir, as if ready for a battle. And at last, near the end of the long day of waiting, the herd of cattle comes into view, filling the width of the drove road.

Now is the time for action. But the villagers rush to get between the Highlanders and their prey, and a sort of battle cannot be avoided. Rob Roy, although angry at their interference, does not want to do them harm, and at his order, the MacGregors use only the flat edges of their swords against the angry farmers. But the farmers are more numerous, and the Highlanders find it hard to push past them. Some are receiving ragged, nasty wounds from the scythes and flails. At a brief command from Rob Roy, the swords are turned edge and point forward, and the clansmen charge, shouting their war cry.

In minutes, the opposition is gone. The farmers have fled to safety, leaving a few dead or wounded on the ground, and nothing stands between Rob Roy and his booty. Nothing except the herdsman. Defending his master's property to the end, he is pierced by a MacGregor sword and falls dying to the ground. The herd is Rob Roy's, and it is speedily driven into the hills.

From the MacGregors' point of view, it is a triumph, a cause for celebration. For the people of Kippen it confirms every bad thing ever said about the Highlanders in general and the MacGregors in particular. To the men in charge of Scotland's affairs, in Stirling Castle and Edinburgh, it brings a new name to the fore, that of young Rob Roy. They will hear it again and again until it drives them to helpless fury.

Chapter Two

At the time Rob Roy was born, the whole Clan MacGregor was in deep trouble. They had powerful neighbours to the west, the Clan Campbell. For more than a hundred years, the MacGregors had been fighting off the Campbells' efforts to take over the land they had always lived in – the wild, hilly district called the Trossachs, not far from the Highland Line, where Highlands and Lowlands meet.

Laws had been passed that forbade the MacGregors using their own name. And unlike any other clan in the Highlands, they could not call their land their own – crafty Campbell chiefs had obtained the title deeds and said the ground was theirs. There was no room for the MacGregors, but they stayed defiantly on.

Rob Roy made his living in several different ways. First, he was a cattle dealer. In the Highlands, young cows were reared and then driven over wild mountain passes and across rivers to market centres such as Crieff or Falkirk, and on from there to the far-off fields of England. Every year, at the start of the season, Rob Roy had to borrow money in order to buy the young cattle. He relied on selling them for a higher price. Then he could pay back the loan and have money left to buy food and other essential goods. But it was not always

easy to get the prices right. Sometimes his profit for the hard work and risk was very small.

But his knowledge of cattle and how to manage them was useful in other ways. When times were hard, it was common for men of one clan to raid the cattle of another clan, or to go down into the Lowlands and "lift" the cattle from the farms there. This of course was stealing, but Rob Roy and the Highlanders did not see it quite like that. They believed that the cattle had always been there and did not belong to anybody. Rob Roy, although he was perhaps the most expert cattle thief ever known in Scotland, also took care to remove cattle only from those who could spare them.

Rob Roy's third means of earning money was also one that is against the law today. Farmers in the wide Lowland valleys would pay him money in order to stop him, and for him to stop others, stealing their cattle or goods. This was called "blackmail", and the word is still used today for obtaining money in this sort of way. But in Rob Roy's time, there were no police. Even the government realised that blackmail was the best way of ensuring peace along the dividing line between Highlands and Lowlands. The farmers who paid Rob Roy could feel safe. Even if their cattle were robbed, Rob Roy would track down the thieves and send the animals back.

Every able-bodied Highlander was expected to be a fighter as well as to possess all the other skills necessary to live among the hills. Young boys practised with sticks, knowing it was not only a game. They lived eagerly for the day when, at sixteen or seventeen, they would be allowed to wear their own swords. One of the many reasons for Rob Roy's special fame was that he was a brilliant sword-fighter. Apart from battles and raids, he fought over twenty duels – single-handed combats with other men. He won them all, except the very last.

Chapter Three

When Rob Roy was a boy, Scotland and England were two separate countries but were ruled by one king, who lived in London. The king's family name was Stuart, and the Stuarts had been kings of Scotland for many years before they also inherited the throne of England. When Rob was seventeen, a very unusual thing happened. King James was forced to leave the country, and his place was taken by two distant relations, the Dutch Prince William of Orange and his wife, Mary. In the Highlands, many of the clans remained loyal to James and the Stuart family. They were called Jacobites, and the MacGregors were among them.

Rob Roy's first battle was when the Jacobites defeated the government army in the Pass of Killiecrankie in Perthshire. For a boy of eighteen it was all very exciting. Rob was almost full-grown. He was not a tall man, but broad and strong with long arms and the confident face of a born leader. He had been brought up as a warrior, like all the clansmen, and to go into battle for his rightful king was to him a duty and a task he was well prepared for. Rob Roy's father had led the MacGregors north to join up with the other Jacobite clans. They were only a few thousand in number, but they were a fast-moving force of trained warriors. The red-coated government soldiers, with their clumsy rifles, were terrified of the Highland charge. It took courage to stand waiting in the front line as the massed clansmen came racing down the hillside in their yellow shirts, shouting Gaelic war cries, brandishing their swords and firing their pistols.

In 1693, Rob got married, to Mary MacGregor, a girl of his own clan whom he had known since he was a boy. Mary MacGregor was a woman of great spirit. When Rob's travels or other difficulties prevented him from visiting the Lowlands to collect his blackmail, she went instead. More than once she would have to stand by and see her home destroyed by soldiers. She and Rob had five sons, as spirited and lively as their parents, and with his many absences, it was largely left to her to bring them up. Their first home was in one of the finest situations in the Highlands, high up on the banks of Loch Lomond. The clan chief bought this land and placed it in trust under Rob Roy.

Chapter Four

When the clan chief died, the new chief was Rob's nephew, a boy of thirteen. Rob became his "tutor". His task was not to teach school lessons to young Gregor of the Black Knee (so called because of a birthmark on one knee) but to teach him how a Highland chief should behave. A chief had to earn the respect of his clansmen. He had to judge their disputes. His house had to be open to them for discussions, entertainment and sometimes refuge. Above all, he had to maintain the honour of the clan. If one MacGregor was insulted, all were insulted. If one was killed, then the chief must see that he was properly avenged. That usually meant more killing. It was a harsh and ancient code, made for a warrior race. And, three hundred years ago, the Highlanders still were warriors who lived by the ancient Celtic traditions.

Once again, in 1693, the name of MacGregor had been forbidden. In public Rob used his mother's name, Campbell. But no change of name protected him in 1695, when he was suddenly arrested on a visit to Glasgow and thrown into prison. For someone used to the freedom of the hills, being jailed was a dreadful experience, not only because of being locked up in a cell but because the cells were small, dark, cold, dirty and full of disease. But Rob Roy was gifted with good luck. For the first, but far from the last time, he escaped from the official clutches. Helped by sympathetic jailers, he was soon back in the Highlands, where the government could not pursue him.

His first son was born in 1695. It was not a good time. Harvests were very poor and the winters were very hard for several years in a row. There was no one to come to the aid of the people of the Highlands. Rob Roy gradually resumed the business of cattle droving, taking great herds down from the Highlands, over the Border hills and deep into England. With the profits from droving and the continuing blackmail, he was able to look after his growing family and to act as the head of the clan while his nephew, Gregor, was too young to be chief.

Scotland was governed in the name of Queen Anne by one of the dukes who owned great tracts of the land. There were four of them, the dukes of Queensberry, Atholl, Argyll and Montrose. They were like greedy children, each trying to get the biggest piece of cake, but far worse because they were wealthy and powerful men whose actions spelt life or death, peace or misery for many thousands of people. Each wanted to be the most powerful man in Scotland, and each plotted against the others.

Rob Roy MacGregor was one of the many men

caught up in the struggle of the dukes. Usually he tried to make sure that he was on good terms with at least one of them. For a long time, the Duke of Montrose had seemed to be his friend. At the start of the cattle-buying season, much of the money he borrowed came from Montrose. But in 1711, a disaster happened. Rob Roy had trusted one of his men with a very large amount of the borrowed money, and the man disappeared with it. When the loss was discovered, Montrose gave him no time or chance to repay. Despite Rob Roy's long record of honest service as a cattle trader, the duke had him officially proclaimed as a thief and announced that anyone who caught him would be well rewarded. Rob soon discovered what Montrose's true aim was.

The Duke of Argyll, known to all the Highlands as Red Iain of the Battles, was a famous soldier who had fought with the English army in Europe. Montrose saw him as a rival. If he could make Queen Anne and her advisers believe that Argyll was friendly to the Jacobites, then Argyll would never receive any government post in Scotland. Rob Roy MacGregor was well known as a leading Jacobite. It was suggested to him by Montrose's agents that if he would swear that Argyll had secretly been in touch with the Jacobite court in France, then the matter of the debt might be forgotten.

Red Rob was a man of honour. To ask him to swear

falsely against another man for a reward was to insult him. He refused. Knowing he would need support, he reported Montrose's offer both to the Duke of Argyll and to the Duke of Atholl.

Montrose proceeded to ruin Rob Roy. He had him put to the horn – publicly named as an outlaw, with long blasts on a horn to summon people to hear. Now anyone was free to kill Rob Roy and claim a reward. Rob had been travelling through England, collecting money from those farmers and dealers who owed it to him. He returned to find his house in ruins, his family homeless, and himself falsely proclaimed as a thief and outlaw. In anger he resolved that the Duke of Montrose would find out that Rob Roy MacGregor was not a man who could ever be frightened off.

Chapter Five

Rob Roy and his family were given a place to live by the old Earl of Breadalbane, at Auchinchisallen in Glen Dochart. Breadalbane cared nothing for the upstart Duke of Montrose. Under the earl's protection he was safe – Montrose could not pursue him into territory held by a Campbell baron. Experienced as a raider since that first expedition to Kippen Muir, Rob Roy was now making a living in the only way he could, by robbing the richer lands south of the Highlands. But he was not a wild and ruthless bandit.

When the Duke of Montrose's rent collectors came to collect the rent from the small farms, they found that Rob Roy's men had been there first. The bandit chief had even signed a receipt on behalf of the duke.

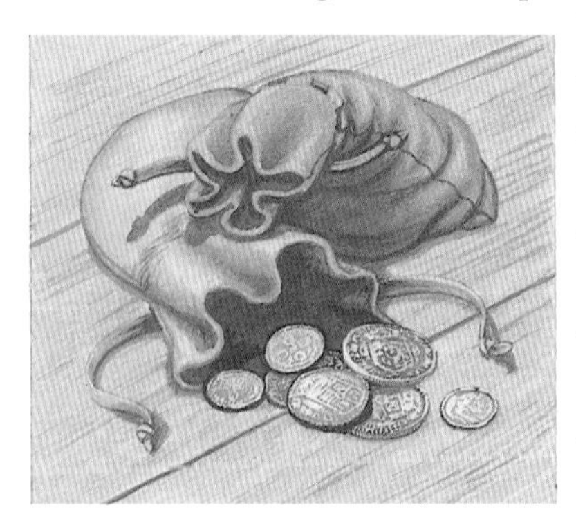

Furious, the duke told his factor to make the farmers pay anyway. But much of the rent was paid in kind (in goods rather than money), and Rob Roy supplied them with stolen grain. There are many stories of how Rob Roy, like a Scottish Robin Hood, used what he had stolen from the rich in order to help the poor.

In 1714, Queen Anne died. There were many in the parliament who would have offered the throne to James Stuart, but they were too slow. Before they could act, the German Prince George of Hanover was brought to London and made king. The angry Jacobites felt cheated and began to prepare for war. The Earl of Mar led them. King George's army was headed by Red Iain of the Battles, who had commanded armies much larger than the one he now led out, as winter fell across the countryside, to face his fellow countrymen, some of them his own friends or relatives.

The battle, when it came, was at Sheriffmuir, above Dunblane, a few miles from Stirling. But for Rob Roy it was hardly a battle at all. He had been sent with two hundred and fifty men to guard a danger-point out to the west, the Fords of Frew, where the River Forth could be crossed.

The rebellion failed, and Rob Roy resumed his raids on Montrose's land. The duke decided it was time to finish with this troublesome rebel. As Rob Roy and his men watched helplessly from the hillside, a troop of Swiss soldiers came and set fire to his house, taking away all the cattle around and anything else that could be carried. There was an exchange of shots, but the MacGregors were outnumbered.

Rob Roy travelled to Inveraray and submitted himself to the justice and protection of the Duke of Argyll. Red Iain was out of favour with the king, but in Argyll it was his word alone that counted. He took the outlawed Jacobite under his protection, and Rob Roy returned to his old home at Inversnaid and built a new house for his family.

A few months later the house was burned to the ground. The vengeful Montrose had arranged for a heavily armed troop to mount a surprise attack. Although the MacGregors were expecting them, they could not prevent the destruction. But the prize the soldiers had been hoping for, Rob Roy himself, eluded them.

He found a new base deep inside the safe haven of Argyll, in Glen Shira, above Loch Fyne, and the remains of his house there can still be seen. Mary and her younger children remained in the MacGregor country, and for several years he saw her for only short periods, each one hazardous.

To show Montrose that he was still dangerous himself, he kidnapped the duke's own factor, or estate manager, and spirited him to an island on Loch Katrine, along with a large amount of the duke's cash. The factor probably expected a knife between his ribs, but a few days later he was set free to report to his master that the Highland barbarians had not ill-treated him in any way.

Chapter Six

Rob Roy relied on two things for his safety The first was the land itself. He knew the country better than anyone. He knew where to hide, where to take a short-cut, where to spring an ambush on the enemy. And like all the Highlanders, he could move across the hills at a great pace, either barefoot or wearing light home-made shoes of deerskin. The second was the people. Although there was a large reward offered for his capture, no one would help the soldiers find him.

With a heavily armed band, the Duke of Montrose stormed a house at Balquhidder where Rob Roy was sheltering and took him prisoner. The duke was jubilant, but by the end of the day Rob Roy was free again. He had been placed on a horse with his hands tied behind his back, but when they came to cross the River Forth, his hands had to be released so that he could hold on to the horse. He was tied to one of his guards, but this was one of the many men who owed Rob a favour. The bond was released or cut, and Rob Roy plunged into the river, letting his plaid float on the surface. It was already getting dark, and he escaped into the twilight. In a mad fury, the duke cracked the guard's skull with a pistol butt.

But even on his own ground and with the protection

of his people, it was a rather desperate and lonely life that Rob Roy was now leading. He wanted to live at peace. As long as he was an outlaw, there could be no safety for him, and continuing trouble for his family and clan. So, when another duke, the Duke of Atholl, proposed a meeting to discuss his submission, Rob Roy was glad to take up the offer. The duke promised him safe-conduct, meaning that he would not be arrested. What Rob Roy did not know was that the duke had no intention of keeping his promise.

To the Duke of Atholl, Rob Roy was a prize to offer to the government. Atholl was not in favour in London. Although he himself supported King George, three of his four sons and most of his clan, the Murrays, supported the Jacobites. Now his plan was to succeed where his rival, the Duke of Montrose, and the army had failed. He would capture the Jacobite bandit, hand him over to justice and be splendidly rewarded.

Trusting in a clan chief's word, Rob Roy walked into the trap. Just as Montrose had done, Atholl wanted Rob Roy to give evidence against the Duke of Argyll. After several years of royal neglect, Argyll was once again rising in favour. If Argyll flourished, Atholl would remain in the wilderness. When Rob Roy refused to betray Argyll, the Duke of Atholl had him overpowered and imprisoned in the tower of Logierait.

Atholl wrote a triumphant letter to the king to say that he had Rob Roy captive. But the duke had not reckoned with Rob Roy. Even as the messenger took the letter, his prisoner was free. A Highlander, Rob's ghillie, or servant, had come to Logierait asking for a message to bring back to Rob's wife, Mary. The guard, over-trusting, let Rob Roy go to the outer door of the guardroom to talk to the man. In a moment Rob had thrust his guard aside, leapt on to the horse the ghillie had brought, and was away.

He remained a generous enemy. One night he took two of Montrose's leading men by surprise (one of them the factor who had once before been kidnapped). They were hunting him, but he simply took their weapons and let them go. He must have regretted his action when one of them, Mungo Graham, caught him on one of his brief stays at home. Placed in the centre of a fast-moving cavalry troop, he was taken away towards Stirling. But as the narrow path rose and fell by the steep side of Loch Lubnaig, the troop had to go in single file and became spread out. Rob Roy picked his time carefully, and in a craggy place, sprang from his horse onto the hillside and disappeared among the trees. Booted soldiers could not hope to match his speed on the ground. He had escaped yet again!

Eventually the pursuit ceased. Rob Roy was at last able to settle down again with his family, and he built another house, deep in the hills at Inverlochlarig Beag,

west of Balquhidder and Loch Voil. There he was once again able to resume the life of a farmer and cattle dealer. But outside events would not let him alone.

The restless Jacobites, always hoping for an opportunity, always believing that they would succeed, had another try in 1719. This uprising is much less famous than those of 1715 and 1745, as it was much smaller and never seemed likely to succeed.

The aim had been to attack from both north and south. A Spanish army was to land in England, and a Highland army was to take control of Scotland. But the Spanish ships heading for England were wrecked or driven back by storms. Meanwhile the Jacobite leaders landed in northwest Scotland with only 300 Spanish troops. The clans were reluctant to fight, but Rob Roy arrived with forty of the MacGregors. It was a hopeless venture. Bombarded from sea and attacked from land, they were defeated in the Battle of Glen Shiel, Rob Roy's last battle for the Stuart cause. He was uninjured and made his way back to the southern Highlands.

Chapter Seven

Once again Rob Roy resumed the life of a Highlander, as it had been when he was a boy and in the time of his fathers before him. Rob maintained the lifestyle of a chieftain, and his fame and personal authority were such that he had as much prestige as if he were a clan chief.

And he found himself written about in a book. Daniel Defoe, better known as the author of *Robinson Crusoe*, wrote a book called *Highland Rogue*, supposedly an account of Rob Roy's doings. Defoe had never met Rob Roy, but the book was very successful and had the effect of turning Rob Roy from being a feared desperado into a famous character. The king who had wanted his head now wanted to meet him. This did not happen, but, almost as unlikely, Rob Roy did meet the Duke of Montrose and made peace with him. Rob agreed that the time had come to stop the cattle raids. In 1725, he at last agreed to be a faithful subject of King George. As with many others, he made this declaration only when he had to, and regarded it as not binding. He certainly remained a Jacobite to the end.

By now he was over sixty, and the great strength that had sustained him throughout a very active life was beginning to weaken. In 1734 he fought his last duel. There was a disagreement between the MacGregors and the Stewarts of Appin (another Jacobite clan) over some land close to Rob Roy's own holding. More than two hundred armed clansmen on each side were ready to do battle to settle the issue. It was Rob Roy's judgement and authority that prevented a bloody fight. He agreed that the Stewarts were in the right, and then, to show that the MacGregors had not backed down through fear, offered to fight any man on the other side. His opponent, much younger, was the first to draw blood – and the first man ever to beat Rob Roy in a fight. He was also the last. Rob knew that his fighting days were over.

Indeed he had only a short time left to live. In December 1734 he had a last visitor, Alexander MacLaren. Rob Roy was ill and weak, but he had himself dressed in his plaid, with his belt around it, and his dirk and pistol. When MacLaren was gone, he said: "It is all over. Put me to bed. Call the piper. Let him play *Cha till me tuille* ('I shall return no more')". As the piper played the slow, lamenting tune, Rob Roy MacGregor died.

You can still see his grave, covered by an ancient carved Celtic stone, in the little churchyard of Balquhidder.